It's a Spoon, Not a Shovel

Caralyn Buehner *Pictures by* Mark Buehner

Dial Books for Young Readers · *New York*

Published by Dial Books for Young Readers
A Division of Penguin Books USA Inc.
375 Hudson Street
New York, New York 10014

Text copyright © 1995 by Caralyn Buehner
Pictures copyright © 1995 by Mark Buehner
All rights reserved
Design by Nancy R. Leo
Printed in Hong Kong
First Edition
1 3 5 7 9 10 8 6 4 2

Library of Congress Catalog Card Number: 93-36293
CIP data available upon request.

*A key to the correct answers can be found on the last page. Also concealed
in the pictures are many little animals — see how many you can find.
One clue — there's a dinosaur, a cat, and a rabbit hiding in each picture.*

*The art for this book was prepared by using oil paints over acrylics.
It was then color-separated and reproduced in red, yellow, blue, and black halftones.*

To Bob, who never shovels,
and reminds us   C. B. and M. B.

ARE YOUR MANNERS MONSTROUS, OR MARVELOUS? Here is a quiz to help you find out. Choose the letter of the answer you think is best. Then look at the picture and see if you can find that same letter hidden in the picture. If you can, you picked the right one!

Let's see how you do!

When Victor Vulture arrives late at the feast, he should say:

     a. "Move it, Buzzard!"

     b. "Excuse me."

     c. "Martians are green."

Marty Mouse has been saving crumbs for weeks to give to Elmer Elephant for his birthday.

Elmer exclaims:

    a. "Your whiskers are twitching."

    b. "Rats! That's not what I wanted!"

    c. "Thank you, Marty!"

Karla Kangaroo is playing hide-and-leap in some bushes. She doesn't see Harold Hyena making mud rabbits and she hops right on top of them!

"Oh!" Karla cries:

    a. "I'm sorry!"

    b. "Clowns have big red noses."

    c. "You stupid hyena! Only pigs play in the mud!"

Harold is saddened at the loss of his bunnies, but graciously replies:

    d. "You have big, stinky feet!"

    e. "That's all right."

    f. "Little red cars go beep, beep, beep."

Arvin Anteater is sucking up ants. His friend Arlo
ambles up to say hello. Arvin offers the next anthill to
Arlo. Arlo moves over promptly and says:

    a. "Outta my way, Blubberbutton!"

    b. "There's a full moon tonight."

    c. "Thank you."

To which Arvin replies:

    d. "Your nose is running."

    e. "You're welcome."

    f. "Dapper diapers."

Wolfgang is bringing his friend Lambert home for dinner. Since Lambert has not met the rest of the pack, Wolfgang performs the introductions. He says, "Brothers, this is Lambert." Then he adds:

   a. "Lambert, this is Howler, Snarler, and Fang."

   b. "Aaaaaaaaaaaaaaaaaarrrrrooooooooooooooooo!"

   c. "Hubba Bubba!"

"Pleased to meet you," Lambert bleats, and the very hungry wolves politely growl:

   d. "Mother's red pajamas."

   e. "Where's the salt and pepper?"

   f. "We're so glad to have you for dinner, Lambert."

Gazing into her sweetheart's eyes while eating an armadillo, Miss Crocodila Jones doesn't notice that she is sitting on her napkin.

Where should she have put her napkin?

    a. On her head.

    b. In her ear.

    c. On her lap.

—— ✺ ——

Trevor Tarantula is anxious to begin eating. His mother places a juicy cricket on his plate. Trevor likes to shake salt on his crickets, and he is tempted to reach across the table and grab the salt shaker. But Trevor has been taught better, so instead he says:

    a. "Have you washed my web yet?"

    b. "Please pass the salt."

    c. "Hot hula hoops!"

✺

Baby Tina digs into her mashed crickets. Daintily Mama Tarantula taps on Tina's foreleg. "Hold your spoon like a pencil, Tina," she murmurs. "Remember, sweetie:

    d. "It's a spoon, not a shovel."

    e. "It's your turn to sleep on the tuffet."

    f. "You're too young to shave your legs."

At the dinner table Walter Warthog's family is spellbound as Walter recounts the tale of his latest narrow escape. Walter takes a big bite of his dinner and continues his story, spraying his family with food. What rule did Walter forget?

    a. Don't step on a crack.

    b. Never talk with your mouth full.

    c. Keep your eyes closed at night.

The Lion family is enjoying a delicious lamb stew. Larry hates to disrupt the meal, but he must leave now for Roaring Practice. He says:

    a. "Lily pads and little frogs."

    b. Nothing.

    c. "Please excuse me."

Melissa Mandrill has finished her dessert before the others. She picks up her fork and uses it to scratch her head, then to clean her fingernails. Poor Melissa has forgotten that a fork is only used to:

    a. Dig in the garden.

    b. Throw at the dart board.

    c. Pick up your food.

A screech from her mother reminds Melissa that when she is finished, she should:

    d. Place her silverware neatly across her plate.

    e. Stand upside down.

    f. Sneeze seven times.

Baby Timmy Snaptooth has his napkin tucked under his chin. When he has swallowed the last juicy morsel, he wipes his hands and mouth on his napkin and places it neatly on the table.

Timmy has shown himself to be:

    a. Courteous, thoughtful, and well trained.

    b. Finished.

    c. Both a. and b.

Cory Cobra has the most exciting news to tell his mother. But when he slithers over, he sees that Mother is talking to Mrs. Python.

Cory is trying hard to be polite, so he decides to:

    a. Hiss.

    b. Eat a rabbit.

    c. Wait quietly.

—— ❧❦❧ ——

Buster Bunny loves to answer the telephone. Usually the calls are for his sister, Bia. Buster says:

    a. "Just a moment, please."

    b. "Black beetles bite."

    c. "Bang! Bang! Bang!"

❧

Of course, if Bia is out nibbling watercress, Buster politely says:

    d. "She's not here, Lettuce-Breath!"

    e. "Windy warblers waddle to Wang's on Wednesday."

    f. "I'm sorry, but Bia can't come to the phone right now. Could I take a message?"

Barney Bull has been polishing his nose ring for hours, but when Hannah Heifer drops all of her daisies in the middle of the road, Barney stops and rumbles:

    a. "Do you need some help?"

    b. "Clumsy Cow!"

    c. "Have you any spare buttermilk?"

How did you do? Did you choose the right letters?
Bravo! You're not alarming, you're *charming*!
Remember:

"Father, Mother, Daughter, Son,
Manners Are for *Everyone*!"

❧ Answer Key ❧

Victor Vulture: The answer "b" is a cactus, upper right.

Marty Mouse: The answer "c" is in the elephant's right eye.

Karla Kangaroo: The answer "a" is in the foliage above the second mud rabbit from the left; answer "e" is next to the left ear of the hyena.

Arvin Anteater: The answer "c" is around the right anteater's left eye; answer "e" is in the foliage, far right.

Wolfgang: The answer "a" is on the sheep's body; answer "f" is above the bottom wolf's snout.

Miss Crocodile: The answer "c" is in the pond to the right of the frog's leg.

Trevor Tarantula: The answer "b" is in a glass; answer "d" is in the wallpaper near the Venus's-flytrap.

Walter Warthog: The answer "b" is on the lip of the warthog.

Lion: The answer "c" is in the soup spoon.

Melissa Mandrill: The answer "c" is in the trees between the parrot and the boy; answer "d" is in the foliage between the tiger and the center mandrill.

Timmy Snaptooth: The answer "c" is in the turtle's hair above the fish earring.

Cory Cobra: The answer "c" is below the right coffee cup and saucer.

Buster Bunny: The answer "a" is on the side of the basket; answer "f" is carved into the picture frame, left.

Barney Bull: The answer "a" is on the front side of the pocketbook.